Honolulu

Honolulu

A Downtown America Book

John Penisten

Dillon Press, Inc.   Minneapolis, MN 55415

This book is dedicated to all the Keiki O Hawaii, the Children of Hawaii, and especially to Janelle and Joelle.

Photographic Acknowledgments

Photos are reproduced through the courtesy of the author, with the exception of the following: the State of Hawaii Archives (p. 23, 30); the U.S.S. *Arizona* Memorial, National Park Service (p. 29); and the Polynesian Cultural Center (p. 40). Cover photo by John Penisten.

Library of Congress Cataloging-in-Publication Data

Penisten, John.
    Honolulu / by John Penisten.
        p.   cm. — (A Downtown America book)
    Includes index.
    Summary: Describes the history, neighborhoods, attractions, and festivals of Honolulu.
    ISBN 0-87518-416-2 : $12.95
    1. Honolulu (Hawaii)—Juvenile literature. [1. Honolulu (Hawaii)]   I. Title.   II. Series.
DU629.H7P39   1989
996.9'31—dc20   89-11973
                                                              CIP
                                                              AC

Dillon Press, Inc., 242 Portland Avenue South
Minneapolis, Minnesota 55415

Printed in the United States of America
1 2 3 4 5 6 7 8 9 10 98 97 96 95 94 93 92 91 90 89

About the Author

An instructor of reading at the University of Hawaii at Hilo, John Penisten has had considerable experience with the Hawaiian Islands. A free-lance photographer and author, he has written one book and has had articles published in journals such as *Aloha* Magazine, *Travel-Holiday,* and the *Los Angeles Herald-Examiner.* In addition to his teaching position, Mr. Penisten is also an editor of publications at the University of Hawaii at Hilo.

Contents

Fast Facts about Honolulu   6

1 The Crossroads of the Pacific   11

2 A Royal Capital   21

3 Where East Meets West   33

4 Finding Fun in Honolulu   43

Places to Visit in Honolulu   56

Honolulu: A Historical Time Line   58

Index   60

Fast Facts about Honolulu

Honolulu: *Crossroads of the Pacific*; translated from Hawaiian, it can mean "fair haven," "sheltered bay," "safe port," or a "meeting place of chiefs"

Location: The Hawaiian island of Oahu in the Pacific Ocean; 2,400 miles (3,864 kilometers) southwest of San Francisco, California; 3,800 miles (6,118 kilometers) southeast of Japan

Area: City, 86 square miles (223 square kilometers); City and County of Honolulu (which includes the entire island of Oahu), 621 square miles (1,608 square kilometers)

Population (1986 estimate*): City, 372,330; City and County of Honolulu, 830,600

Major Population Groups: Asians, whites, native Hawaiians or part Hawaiians

Altitude: *Highest*, Mount Kaala, 4,020 feet (1,226 meters); *Lowest*, sea level

Climate: Average temperature is 72°F (22°C) in January, 80°F (26°C) in July; average annual precipitation is 25 inches (62 centimeters), but this varies with elevation

Founding Date: Discovered in 1794; declared the capital of the Kingdom of Hawaii on August 31, 1850; incorporated as the City and County of Honolulu in 1907

City Flag: The City and County of Honolulu has no official city flag

City Seal: A star in the center of the shield represents the Hawaiian monarchy; the upper right and lower left quarters of the shield show a Hawaiian *pulo'ulo'u* — a tapa cloth-covered ball on a stick carried before a chief to mean authority, protection, and tabu; red, white, and blue stripes in the other quarters are also symbols of the monarchy; the shield is surrounded by Diamond Head and a canoe on one side,

*U.S. Bureau of the Census 1988 population estimates available in fall 1989; official 1990 census figures available in 1991-92.

and by the Pali Highway leading up to the Koolau Mountains on the other; the rising sun above the shield represents a new beginning

Form of Government: Mayor-council; a mayor and nine council members are each elected to govern the island for four-year terms

Important Industries: Tourism, food processing, agriculture, retail, foreign trade

Festivals and Parades

January: Chinese New Year's celebration; Narcissus Festival

February: Cherry Blossom Festival

March: Japanese Girls' Day; St. Patrick's Day parade; Prince Kuhio Day

April: Buddha's Birthday celebration

May: Lei Day; Japanese Boys' Day; Philippines Cultural Day

June: King Kamehameha Day; Japanese Obon Festival

July: Okinawa Festival

August: Kapiolani Park Hula Festival

September: Aloha Week parade and celebration

October: Kanikapila Hawaiian Music Festival

December: Buddhist Day of Enlightenment; Festival of Trees

For further information about festivals and parades, see agencies listed on page 57.

United States

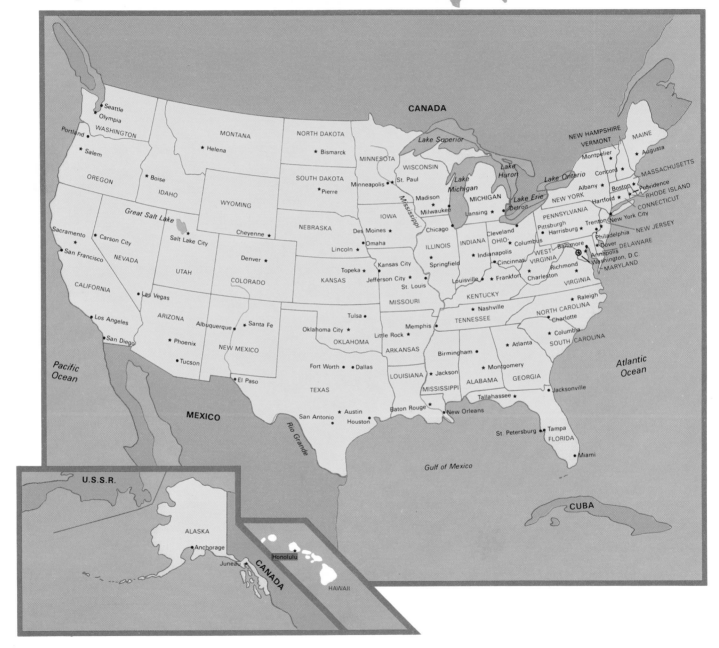

CANADA

Seattle
Olympia
WASHINGTON
Portland

Salem

OREGON

MONTANA

Helena

Boise

IDAHO

NORTH DAKOTA

Bismarck

SOUTH DAKOTA

Pierre

WYOMING

Cheyenne

MINNESOTA

Lake Superior

WISCONSIN

St. Paul

Minneapolis

Madison

Milwaukee

Lake Michigan

MICHIGAN

Lansing

Lake Huron

Lake Ontario

Lake Erie

Detroit

NEW HAMPSHIRE
VERMONT
Montpelier
Concord

MAINE

Augusta

MASSACHUSETTS

Boston
Providence

Albany
Hartford
RHODE ISLAND

NEW YORK
CONNECTICUT

Great Salt Lake

Sacramento
Carson City

San Francisco

NEVADA

CALIFORNIA

Salt Lake City

UTAH

Las Vegas

Los Angeles

San Diego

Denver

COLORADO

Las Vegas

ARIZONA

Phoenix

Tucson

Albuquerque

Santa Fe

NEW MEXICO

El Paso

NEBRASKA

IOWA

Des Moines

Lincoln

Omaha

KANSAS

Topeka

Kansas City

Jefferson City

Chicago

ILLINOIS

Springfield

St. Louis

MISSOURI

Tulsa

Oklahoma City

OKLAHOMA

Fort Worth

Dallas

TEXAS

San Antonio

Austin

Houston

Rio Grande

Little Rock

ARKANSAS

Memphis

Mississippi

INDIANA

Indianapolis

Cincinnati

OHIO

Columbus

Cleveland

Louisville

Frankfort

KENTUCKY

Nashville

TENNESSEE

Birmingham

Montgomery

ALABAMA

MISSISSIPPI

Jackson

Baton Rouge

LOUISIANA

New Orleans

PENNSYLVANIA

Pittsburgh

Harrisburg

WEST VIRGINIA

Charleston

Richmond

VIRGINIA

Trenton
New York City
Philadelphia
NEW JERSEY
Dover
DELAWARE
Baltimore
Annapolis
Washington, D.C.
MARYLAND

Raleigh

NORTH CAROLINA

Charlotte

Columbia

SOUTH CAROLINA

Atlanta

GEORGIA

Tallahassee

Jacksonville

St. Petersburg

Tampa

FLORIDA

Miami

Atlantic Ocean

Pacific Ocean

MEXICO

Gulf of Mexico

CUBA

U.S.S.R.

ALASKA

Anchorage

Juneau

CANADA

Honolulu

HAWAII

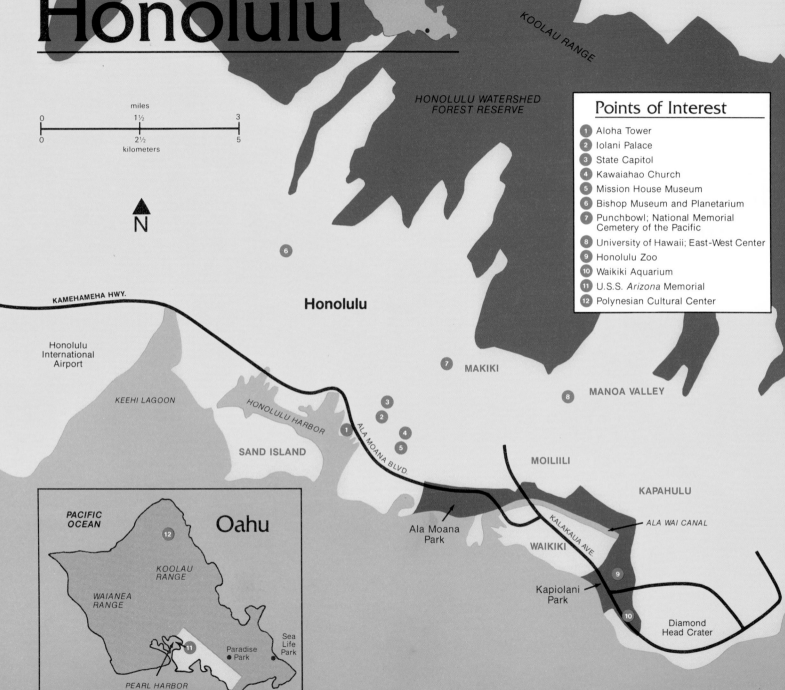

Honolulu

KOOLAU RANGE

HONOLULU WATERSHED
FOREST RESERVE

miles
0   1½   3
0   2½   5
kilometers

N

Points of Interest

1 Aloha Tower
2 Iolani Palace
3 State Capitol
4 Kawaiahao Church
5 Mission House Museum
6 Bishop Museum and Planetarium
7 Punchbowl; National Memorial
   Cemetery of the Pacific
8 University of Hawaii; East-West Center
9 Honolulu Zoo
10 Waikiki Aquarium
11 U.S.S. *Arizona* Memorial
12 Polynesian Cultural Center

KAMEHAMEHA HWY.

Honolulu

Honolulu
International
Airport

KEEHI LAGOON

HONOLULU HARBOR

ALA MOANA BLVD.

SAND ISLAND

MAKIKI

MANOA VALLEY

MOILIILI

KAPAHULU

Ala Moana
Park

KALAKAUA AVE.

ALA WAI CANAL

WAIKIKI

Kapiolani
Park

Diamond
Head Crater

Oahu

PACIFIC
OCEAN

KOOLAU
RANGE

WAIANEA
RANGE

Paradise
Park

Sea
Life
Park

PEARL HARBOR

1

The Crossroads of the Pacific

Honolulu, Hawaii, is one of America's most colorful cities. In some areas, shimmering fields of emerald green sugarcane lead down to the seashore. In other places, mountain peaks reach toward the sky. From the air, it appears that the green earth of Honolulu and the blue sky are separated only by a curl of the white surf along sandy beaches.

When most people think of Honolulu, they think of the word *aloha*. Aloha is a special Hawaiian word with many meanings, depending on how and when it is used. It can mean hello or good-bye, or it can be an expression of love or goodwill.

In the Hawaiian language, Honolulu, too, can have many meanings. Whether they call it a "fair haven," "safe port," "sheltered bay," or even a "meeting place of chiefs," most

Honolulu is a combination of high-rise hotels and tropical rain forests.

Honolulu is home to many different ethnic and religious groups, including Buddhists, who meet in temples such as this one.

Honolulans wouldn't live anywhere else. They have *aloha aina* for their home—a deep sense of love and respect for the land and the sea, and for all life.

Located on the island of Oahu, one of the eight main islands forming the Hawaiian Island chain in the Pacific Ocean, Honolulu is the capital of Hawaii. It is 2,400 miles (3,864 kilometers) southwest of San Francisco, California, and 3,800 miles (6,118 kilometers) southeast of Japan. Its nearest neighbors are the islands of Tahiti and Tonga, and the Samoas, another Pacific island group 2,000 miles (3,200 kilometers) to the south.

Officially, Honolulu covers the whole island of Oahu, along with several small offshore islands, and is known as the City and County of Honolulu. Usually, though, only the large, busy, and crowded area on the southeastern coast of Oahu is called Honolulu.

Honolulu is home to more than 830,000 people, and its population continues to grow. Honolulu's people are different from those in any other American city. More than four of every ten Honolulans are Asian— either recent immigrants, or descendants of the early settlers of Honolulu, who came from China, Japan, Korea, and other Asian countries. Almost 30 percent of today's Honolulans can trace their heritage back to the people who discovered the Hawaiian Islands. These explorers from islands in the South Pacific Ocean sailed to Hawaii in large, hand-made canoes. Oahu was one of the islands on which they built villages.

Since the days of the first settlers, Honolulu has grown from a quiet tropical port into a busy center for business and tourism. In fact, tourism is Honolulu's largest source of income. The Honolulu International Airport handles millions of passengers each year—some tourists, and some who wish to immigrate to the United States. Of those who work in Honolulu, more than half have jobs in a business which is designed to serve tourists.

Because of its location between Asia and the United States, Honolulu is known as the Crossroads of the Pacific. It is a stopover for cargo and

passenger ships, as well as airlines. Honolulu is also the center of U.S. armed forces in the Pacific region, and is the home of Pearl Harbor, an important military base. Military spending is the second largest source of income in the city.

Honolulu's leading manufacturing industry is food processing. During the past century, many plants have been built to process pineapple and sugarcane grown on the island.

These two crops have been very important in the development of Honolulu. Early residents depended on pineapple and sugarcane plantations to supply jobs and food. The variety of ethnic groups in Honolulu today is due partly to these plantations: owners of the large farms had to "import" workers from Asian and Pacific countries because there weren't enough people in Honolulu to do all the work.

Honolulu's economy depends on crops and products in addition to pineapple and sugarcane. Taro, for example, is also grown in Honolulu. This starchy root is ground into a paste and used to make poi, a Hawaiian food. Sweet-tasting fruits, such as papayas, are grown in the countryside of Honolulu, and so are beautiful flowers such as the vanda orchid and the heart-shaped anthurium.

Sugarcane, pineapple, and other tropical foods grow well in Honolulu because of the city's location just south of the Tropic of Cancer. This is an imaginary line circling the globe

Both passenger and cargo ships dock in busy Honolulu Harbor.

that marks the northern boundary of the tropical zone. Most places south of this line are very hot. Ocean breezes, though, keep Honolulu's temperature comfortable. On most days, the temperature ranges from 71°F to 80°F (22°C to 27°C).

The city's geography also influences the weather. Rainstorms sweep over the 4,000-foot (1,220-meter) Koolau and Waianae mountain ranges of central Oahu. Because of these mountain ranges, the central valley that lies between them receives the heavy rainfall needed to grow pineapple and sugarcane. On some days, it may be raining in the mountains and central valley, while the lowlands along the coast are dry and sunny.

Honolulu's scenery has as much

Sugarcane is one of Honolulu's most important crops.

Pineapple fields dot the central valley of Oahu.

variety as its weather. The city is an unusual blend of the modern and the undeveloped. Hotels, restaurants, shopping malls, and factories are surrounded by tropical rain forests, golden beaches, green parks, beautiful waterfalls, and monuments to the city's royal past. Honolulu is the only American city to have been the capital of a kingdom.

Before the late 1800s, Hawaii was known as the Royal Kingdom of Hawaii. Iolani Palace, the home of the kingdom's royalty, was built between

Some modern Honolulans still perform the hula, an important traditional dance, on special occasions.

1870 and 1880 by King Kalakaua, and still stands today in downtown Honolulu.

Warm weather, beautiful beaches, good food, and friendly people attract 6 million tourists to Honolulu each year. Hawaiians come here, too—four of every five Hawaiians choose to live in Honolulu. With so many people in one area, there are problems with overcrowding, especially in the popular Waikiki area. But city residents are trying to find solutions to meet everyone's needs.

The number of people who have chosen to live in Honolulu has also affected the island's wildlife. Animals that once roamed the island freely are now usually seen only in the Honolulu Zoo. On rare occasions, though, a lucky Honolulan might be able to see the Hawaiian I'o (a hawk), the koloa duck, or the Nene goose, the state bird of Hawaii.

The animals in Honolulu are an important part of the city's beauty. The Hawaiian thrush, Hawaiian crow, Hawaiian creeper, and other tropical birds live in the rain forests of Honolulu, while animals such as the gecko, a small lizard, roam the city parks. The gecko also lives in homes and public buildings. This lizard is harmless and eats only insects, but it can give a scare to anyone not used to it.

Honolulu is also home to the Giant Neotropical toad, or as it's called locally, the bufo. This big toad hops around chasing insects, and when it is happiest—during rainshowers—its loud croak can be heard in parks and gardens around the city.

Honolulans take advantage of the natural beauty of their city all year long. Residents can shop in the outdoor markets in Chinatown, stroll through the city's many parks, or take a drive through Oahu's central valley.

In Hawaiian, Oahu means "gathering place." With its year-round sunshine and activities, it is not surprising that Honolulu is the place where Hawaiians and tourists meet. From its beginnings as cooled lava almost 30 million years ago, Honolulu has become a lovely, energetic city—an island of bright green set in the vast blue waters of the Pacific Ocean.

2

A Royal Capital

The Hawaiian Islands were formed over millions of years by volcanoes on the ocean floor erupting and sending out streams of lava. As the lava cooled, it slowly built up until it reached the surface of the ocean and broke through, forming the islands. Scientists think that the first eruption began about 30 million years ago beneath the small island of Kure Atoll, far to the northwest of Honolulu. For-

tunately for Hawaiians, there are only two active volcanoes today. Both of these, Mauna Loa and Kilauea, are on the island of Hawaii, the southernmost island in the state.

The first people to settle in Hawaii were Polynesians. These ancient sailors left their homes in the South Pacific to sail across the ocean in large, hand-carved canoes with sails made from coconut fronds. They were

Iolani Palace in downtown Honolulu is one sign of the city's royal past.

searching for a mythical homeland called *Hawaiki*, the place from which they thought their ancestors had come.

Along with live chickens, pigs, and a variety of plants from their own islands, the Polynesians brought their ways of life and religion with them. The people worshipped many gods and goddesses. Their religion was based on a system of *kapus*, or tabus, which meant that many actions and types of behavior were not allowed.

The settlers also brought a strong sense of conservation with them. The Hawaiians loved and respected the land they lived on and were one of the first peoples to preserve and protect animal and plant life. The *alii*, or royalty, limited the number and kinds of fish and game that could be caught, and only allowed people to hunt and fish at certain times of the year.

If a tree was cut down, the law required the citizens to plant another one. Hawaiians were also among the first peoples to zone their land. Under this plan, certain parts of Honolulu and Oahu were used for buildings, and other parts were left in their natural state. The results of this conservation can be seen in today's Honolulu, where areas of the city and county are officially set aside as "open spaces."

Early Hawaiians used the island of Oahu, and the village that formed on its southeastern coast, as a place to gather and find ways to solve their problems. Honolulu, as the village would later be called, was a natural meeting place because its harbor was easy to enter.

In 1789, the trading ship, *Eleanora*, brought the first Chinese immigrants to Honolulu. The trader was on its way from China to North America when it stopped in Honolulu for the winter. Many of the 45 Chinese crew members decided to stay on the tropical island. Since that time, thousands more Chinese have immigrated to Honolulu, and they remain an important part of the city's population.

In the early 1790s, Oahu was the site of a civil war among Hawaiians. King Kamehameha I of the island of Hawaii wanted to unite all the islands under his rule. After a long and bloody fight, he succeeded in conquering

An early drawing of King Kamehameha *nui* (the Great).

Oahu in 1795, and the Kingdom of Hawaii was formed soon afterward.

In 1794, William Brown, the captain of a British merchant ship, discovered the tiny bay of Kou on Oahu's southern coast. Kou was the only harbor at the time that he could enter. The bay offered a safe place to rest and was a beautiful area, so Brown named it "Fair Haven." In time, the Hawaiian name for Fair Haven—Honolulu—replaced the previous name on maps and charts.

As more and more sailors and merchants heard of Brown's discovery, Honolulu grew. It became an important center for trading sandalwood in the 1800s, and later was used as a chief base for whaling ships in the Pacific. The tiny village grew into an important port filled with sailing ships and traders of all kinds. The sailors would stop in Honolulu to rest, repair their ships, or buy supplies. Even then, Honolulu was thought of as a good refueling stop on the routes from Asia to America.

Many of the sailors and merchants who stopped there for a rest liked the port so well, they stayed, adding to the growing population. By 1819, the town was home to Chinese, French, Italian, British, Spanish, Scotch, and American people.

In May of that year, something happened that would change life in Honolulu, and all of Hawaii, forever. King Kamehameha I died, and his son Kamehameha II took over. Because he was not a very good leader, most

of the decisions about the kingdom were made by Kamehameha I's favorite wife, Kaahumanu. She didn't believe that men and women should be treated in different ways, so she changed many laws that she felt were unfair, and allowed all the people in the kingdom greater freedom.

When New England missionaries arrived in 1820, Hawaiian rules and life-styles were still changing. At first, the missionaries were uncomfortable in the tropical climate and were shocked by the strange habits and religion of the Hawaiian people. In time, though, the missionaries converted many Honolulans and other Hawaiians to Christianity. They were helped partly by Kaahumanu, who was one of the first Hawaiians to con-vert. The missionaries built many schools and churches. One that still stands today is the Kawaiahao Church in Honolulu, made from 140,000 coral blocks.

To many Honolulans of the time, the missionaries were troublesome foreigners. They outlawed such things as the hula (a native dance), leis (necklaces of fresh flowers), and kite flying. Fortunately, these beautiful Hawaiian customs were never lost and are still a part of the islands' heritage.

As Honolulu continued to expand, farming grew, too. The growth of large sugarcane and pineapple plantations led to the racial mix of today's Honolu. Many workers were needed to plant the crops, harvest them, and then process them in the new plants

Built by New England missionaries, Kawaiahao Church is now a historical museum.

around the island. Thousands of immigrants came from Japan, China, and other countries to work in the fields and processing plants.

Unfortunately for many Hawaiian natives, these newcomers brought more than a willingness to work.

They brought diseases to which the Hawaiians had never before been exposed. Many of the islands' people died from the new diseases.

Nevertheless, the city of Honolulu continued to grow. In 1845, King Kamehameha III moved the government from Lahaina, Maui, to Honolulu. In 1850, he declared the city the permanent capital of the Royal Kingdom of Hawaii.

Honolulu became even more important when, in 1887, King Kalakaua, a descendant of Kamehameha, gave the United States the right to use Pearl Harbor as a naval station. Pearl Harbor lies a short distance to the west of downtown Honolulu. The new naval base brought a large number of people, many of them Americans, to the city and surrounding areas.

After King Kalakaua died, his sister Liliuokalani became queen of the kingdom. Her reign, though, was cut short in 1893 when a revolution, led by nine Americans and four Europeans, removed her from control. A year later, they formed the Republic of Hawaii and elected Sanford Dole as its president. Dole's family would later start the well-known Dole pineapple company.

During this time, the demand for pineapples and sugar was growing in the United States, and plantation owners in Honolulu were becoming very powerful. These American businessmen gained control of the Republic of Hawaii. The plantation owners also controlled agriculture and food processing—then Hawaii's largest industries. They wanted Oahu and the other Hawaiian islands to become a part of the United States because it would allow them to earn more money from their crops and food processing plants.

Until recently, Hawaii's economy was controlled by a few large companies which had been started by the major plantation and factory owners in Hawaii.

In the late 1890s, the United States government also had an interest in Hawaii. U.S. leaders knew Honolulu had a good harbor, and they wanted to expand their military posts in the islands. Despite protests from many Hawaiians, the United States officially declared Hawaii an American possession. On June 14, 1900, Hawaii became a territory of the United States. Seven years later, officials formed the City and County of Honolulu. From that time on, the city of Honolulu and the county of Honolulu shared the same borders and the same government, making the island of Oahu one big community.

During the 1900s, the United States created many new military bases in the islands, most of them in the downtown Honolulu area. The increased military activity helped increase the population of Honolulu to 137,000 people in 1930. Still, at this time, the city wasn't known to most Americans. That changed on December 7, 1941, when Japanese planes bombed Pearl Harbor. Not only did this force the United States to enter World War II, it also brought Honolulu to the attention of the world. Many soldiers who had moved to the city to work on the naval, air force, and army bases stayed when the war ended.

The U.S.S. *Arizona* in 1941 as it sinks into Pearl Harbor.

A Honolulu newspaper headline announces statehood for Hawaii on August 21, 1959.

After World War II, some important changes took place among Honolulu's various ethnic groups. The Japanese, Chinese, and other Asians had been kept out of business and politics since Hawaii became a U.S. territory. In some cases, newly arrived Americans had forced Asian leaders to leave their jobs. Following the war, though, Honolulans of Asian origin again became leaders in government and industry.

On August 21, 1959, the United States Congress admitted Hawaii to the Union, making it the 50th state. Honolulu, once capital of a royal kingdom, now became the state capital. The city grew quickly as air transportation between the United States mainland and Hawaii improved, bringing more and more people to see the new state. Hotels and apartment highrises were built where before there had been nothing but swamp and rain forest.

During the 1960s, major Honolulu companies grew and opened new offices in several foreign countries. As interest in Honolulu increased, new companies from the United States mainland and Asia moved to Honolulu. Airlines, hotels, tour and travel companies, real estate firms, retail stores, and banking and finance companies all began to open offices in Honolulu and other Hawaiian cities.

Honolulu's growth continued into the 1970s and 1980s when television shows such as "Hawaii Five-0," starring Jack Lord, and "Magnum, P.I.," starring Tom Selleck, made the city better known to millions of people.

Damage done by Hurricane Iwa in 1982 slowed the pace of Honolulu's growth, but didn't stop immigrants and visitors from coming to the city. Today, Honolulu's people, food, and beautiful landscape all combine to make it one of the most popular places for tourists in the Pacific Ocean.

3

Where East Meets West

For Honolulans, the August day in 1959 when they became a part of the United States was a proud one. Most Hawaiians were eager to become American citizens, and many showed their happiness in parties around the islands. People of all races came together to celebrate.

Honolulu is often called a true melting pot because its population is made up almost entirely of "foreign-ers." Only about one in every four Honolulans is a native Hawaiian or part Hawaiian.

In most large cities, different ethnic groups tend to gather in separate areas. In Honolulu, this is not the case. Here, neighborhoods are made up of many different groups. Each group is proud of its individual heritage, though, and this ethnic pride appears in the different restaurants

A group of Honolulu students play traditional Japanese instruments.

Outdoor markets in Chinatown sell everything from cucumbers to kiwi fruit.

and shops around the city, as well as in the people themselves.

Even in Chinatown, with its variety of shops and markets, different people live together. Chinatown was one of the first places to be settled in Honolulu. It has many specialty stores, bakeries, open vegetable and meat markets, and restaurants.

Chinatown is located next to the modern high-rises of busy downtown Honolulu, the heart of the city. Its wide streets, lined with palm trees, are usually filled with cars. It is here that the city's history can be seen in buildings such as Iolani Palace, Kawaiaho Church, and the bronze statue of King Kamehameha I in front of the Aliiolani Hale Judiciary Building. On the grounds of Iolani Palace are the Iolani barracks, which once served as a home to the royal guards, and Iolani bandstand, where Hawaii's governors are sworn in.

One famous Honolulu landmark is Diamond Head Crater (also called Mount Leahi), an inactive volcano. Clustered around the base of Diamond Head are the neighborhoods of Moiliili, Kapahulu, and Waikiki. Moiliili has many broad avenues, shops, and commercial buildings, along with a few small apartment buildings. Many Moiliili and Kapahulu residents work in neighboring Waikiki.

Waikiki is more than just a beach and a tourist center. One of Honolulu's busiest and most crowded neighborhoods, it includes several hundred high-rise hotels and apartment buildings. City and state planners are presently discussing ways to slow the growth of the Waikiki area. Like most Honolulans, they want to preserve the natural beauty of their city.

On the east side of Diamond Head are Honolulu's wealthier neighborhoods—Waialae and Kahala. There are few high-rise buildings here, and the area has many expensive, well-tended homes.

Beyond the coastal flatlands,

Soldiers and sailors killed in Pacific battles are buried in the Punchbowl crater.

some of Honolulu's older neighborhoods extend up the ridges and valleys in the foothills of the Koolau Mountains. These communities include Makiki, which surrounds Punchbowl, a volcanic crater that once served as a place of sacrifice for the Hawaiians. Today, it is the National Memorial Cemetery of the Pacific, where 26,000 American soldiers and sailors are buried.

Behind Punchbowl is Tantalus Drive, which twists and turns up and down lovely, tree-lined slopes and

Diamond Head Crater rises behind the Honolulu communities of Moiliili and Kapahulu.

valleys of Mount Tantalus. Lookouts provide beautiful views of downtown Honolulu, Diamond Head Crater, the Waikiki area, and the suburbs of Honolulu. Tantalus Drive is one of Honolulu's most scenic drives.

Nearby Manoa Valley is a residential neighborhood with narrow streets and handsome older homes. Most of the people in the valley either work or are students at the University of Hawaii at Manoa. This university is noted for its special Asian and Pacific study programs.

Other neighborhoods in Honolulu, such as Aina Haina, Niu Valley, Hawaii Kai, and Kalama Valley, are farther from the downtown area. These communities are home to Honolulans who must commute to the city center to work each day.

On Oahu's north shore, east coast, and west coast are several other small towns and settlements. Many grew and developed around the sugarcane and pineapple plantations.

The people who worked on the plantations came from many different countries, and each group spoke a different language. Today, a number of those languages are still spoken by modern Honolulans. Although most residents speak English, there are many Pacific and Asian languages, too. Some of Honolulu's newspapers are printed in Japanese, Chinese, or Korean to serve residents who prefer to read in one of these languages.

Also, Honolulu is the only Amer-

The Korea Studies Building at the East-West Center is only a small part of this cultural and business center.

ican city with separate Chinese, Japanese, and Portuguese chambers of commerce to help meet the needs of all ethnic groups.

To promote better relations between the East and West, the U.S. Congress created the East-West Center on the University of Hawaii at Manoa campus in 1960. Each year, more than 2,000 students and other representatives from Asia and the Pacific region attend meetings and classes at the center. They work to find solutions to social and economic

problems. The East-West Center is very important in the growth of trade and commerce in the Pacific.

In addition to being a business center for Asia and the Pacific, Honolulu is also home to the Polynesian Cultural Center, which celebrates Hawaii's rich heritage. The center features six villages like those found on the islands of Fiji, Tonga, Samoa, New Zealand, and Hawaii. Visitors to the center can see what life was like on the islands when they were first discovered.

Honolulu's schools, too, are designed to remind children of their heritage. In addition to the subjects studied in other American schools, Honolulu's children learn about the history of the Hawaiian Islands. One

entire year of elementary school is reserved for the study of Polynesian culture and customs.

This program lets Hawaiian children develop a strong knowledge of their home and its people. Teachers and parents hope the young people will gain respect for the land and work to preserve it as they grow older. The special classes also help students understand the different groups of people that make up Honolulu.

On this mid-Pacific island of rain forests and mountains, East and West—as well as North and South—mix and meet each day in one of America's most beautiful melting pots.

At the Polynesian Cultural Center, these Honolulans demonstrate traditional Tahitian dances.

4

Finding Fun in Honolulu

Honolulu is the gathering place of many Hawaiians, the place to go to meet friends, or to walk or sunbathe on the beach. It is also the place most of Hawaii's tourists visit each year, adding to the constant flow of activity.

Waikiki is one of Honolulu's busiest areas. The black figure of Diamond Head, a huge, circular crater with jagged sloping walls 760 feet (232 meters) tall, provides a beautiful backdrop to the white sand and blue seas.

A generation ago, this area was a deserted swamp few people knew about. Since Hawaii became a state, though, Waikiki has become the center of Hawaii's tourist industry. Along with Kalakaua Avenue, with its rows of hotels, shopping arcades, and restaurants, Waikiki is the center of activity in a lively area that is active day and night.

The golden sand and clear blue sea of Waikiki attract both Hawaiians and visitors to Honolulu.

Outrigger canoes such as this one are similar to those used by early Honolulans.

The beach and the sea play an important role in Waikiki. Here, people can swim in the ocean or relax in the sand. Honolulans enjoy surfing, sail boarding, snorkeling, underwater diving, and parasailing. They can also explore the reefs in the bay, paddle an outrigger canoe, ride a water-bike, or enjoy a cruise in a glass-bottomed boat. If they get tired, they just lean back and relax in the warm Pacific Ocean breezes.

Honolulu has many other beautiful beaches to enjoy, too: Hanauma

Bay, Sandy Beach, Makapuu Beach, and Waimanalo Beach. The famous surfing beaches—Sunset and Bonzai Pipeline, Waimea Bay, Rocky Point, and Laniakea—attract surfers from around the world. During the winter, the waves in some of these areas can be as high as 40 feet (12 meters).

Surfing, swimming, and sunbathing aren't the only activities Honolulans enjoy. Next to the Waikiki area lies Kapiolani Park, which is filled with tropical greenery and playgrounds. Children in Honolulu play soccer, baseball, basketball, and volleyball here. On days when it's not too windy, they may have to watch for a model airplane flying around the park, or duck their head to avoid a passing frisbee or dipping kite.

The Honolulu Zoo and Waikiki Aquarium are both in Kapiolani Park. The zoo features a variety of animals from countries around the world, as does the aquarium. The aquarium also has a display of tropical marine life found along Hawaii's coastline.

For an even more striking look at Hawaii's marine life, Sea Life Park provides a close-up view of hundreds of fish. A spiral staircase winds down and around a giant aquarium, where visitors can look into the depths of underwater Hawaii. Here, they can see the fabulous coral reefs, watch the many forms of reef life, and even see a shark or a manta ray glide quietly by. Sea Life Park also features performances by trained

Visitors to Sea Life Park are able to see almost every type of marine life found off Honolulu's shores.

dolphins, seals, water birds, and other marine animals.

Paradise Park, in Manoa Valley, is home to many brightly colored tropical birds. It is a peaceful park of streams, waterfalls, ponds, curving pathways, and lush tropical rain forests. It is also the home of hundreds of forest birds, such as macaws, cockatoos, and parrots.

Near downtown Honolulu is the Bishop Museum. It is one of the best places in the world to find out about the history, life-styles, and people of the Pacific Ocean countries. The museums's planetarium includes a program about the stars and planets and how they influenced the lives of the Pacific peoples. There are many special shows and programs throughout the year to add to the museum's attractions.

Near Iolani Palace, which shows how the Hawaiian kings and queens lived, is the Mission Houses Museum. Here, visitors learn about the history of Honolulu and its relationship with the missionaries.

A few blocks from the city center, the Aloha Tower rises above the harbor's piers. It offers a stunning view of Honolulu Harbor and the city itself.

Diamond Head Crater offers yet another look at Honolulu. From a lookout perched on the crater's edge, people can get a bird's-eye view of areas of the city along the coast. To get to the lookout, visitors must take a 45-minute hike up a winding trail inside the crater. At one point, the trail passes through a long, dark tunnel. When it finally comes out at the lookout, though, the view makes the trip well worth the effort.

The Diamond Head lookout was once used by the military in World War II. The presence, past and present, of U.S. armed forces can be seen in several places.

At Pearl Harbor, Honolulans and visitors can see the memorial to the U.S.S. *Arizona*, which was sunk on December 7, 1941. Rather than trying

This colorful Chinatown restaurant is one of many ethnic restaurants in Honolulu.

to remove the ship, the navy left it in the harbor to honor the crew members killed when the ship was attacked. The navy operates free ferry boat rides to the Arizona Memorial from the Honolulu visitor's center. Located in Pearl Harbor, the long, white memorial has an observation deck which allows people to see the wreck of the ship in the water.

Honolulu is a wonderful place to try a variety of new and different foods. When Hawaii's many ethnic groups left their homelands, they brought with them their native recipes. Today, Honolulans can sample Japanese, Chinese, Filipino, Korean, Portuguese, Polynesian, and many other types of food all in one place. Even the Honolulu McDonalds restaurants serve local foods, such as Oriental noodles and salads, and spicy Portuguese sausage and eggs, along with their regular menu.

A good place to try some interesting food is at a take-out cafe or restaurant that serves plate lunches. The local menus include Japanese saimin (noodles), sushi (raw fish), and teriyaki beef; Korean chicken and spiced beef; Chinese egg rolls and manapua (steamed buns); or Hawaiian laulau (spiced fish, chicken, or beef wrapped in leaves), lomilomi

salmon (spicy fish), and poi (mashed taro root). One local favorite comes from the American southwest—chili and rice. There are many more ethnic foods, all offering an interesting choice for anyone who can't decide what to eat.

On days when the sun may get too hot, Honolulans and visitors can enjoy shaved ice from one of the many stands throughout the city. Shaved ice is what people from the mainland call a snow cone. But in Honolulu, it comes with tropical fruit-flavored syrups. Choices include banana, pineapple, guava, mango, passion fruit, and more. Shaved ice can also be topped with a scoop of ice cream. As they say in Honolulu, it is *ono* (delicious).

In addition to the variety of foods it offers, Honolulu has many festivals and ethnic celebrations each year. In January, the Narcissus Festival is held in old Chinatown, celebrating the traditional Chinese New Year. The festival includes a Queen Pageant, a coronation ball, and a colorful parade of floats, marchers, and groups dressed in Chinese costumes.

The highlight of the parade is the appearance of the Chinese lion, a long swirling float carried over the heads of several people. The lion usually has a fierce-looking head and must be rewarded with donations of money placed in its mouth. The money is then donated to charity.

While making its way through the streets of Chinatown, the lion dances to clashing cymbals, banging drums, and the popping of thousands of firecrackers.

During the Narcissus Festival, there is a general open house in Chinatown. Cafes, noodle shops, and Chinese markets set up sidewalk booths so people can sample all of the authentic Chinese foods that are available. Some booths display Chinese history in Honolulu, and arts and crafts.

Another important cultural celebration is the annual Japanese Cherry Blossom Festival, held from late February through early March. This celebration features Japanese folk dancing, music, arts and crafts, the Japanese tea ceremony, cooking demonstrations, and even a fashion show.

A young Honolulan enjoys a shaved ice treat.

Dressed in kimonos, these Honolulan girls celebrate their city's Japanese heritage.

During the festival, several young Japanese-American women compete for the title of the Cherry Blossom Queen and its grand prize of a college scholarship. All contestants must be able to speak Japanese, and must know about Japanese culture, dance, and customs.

Honolulans with Japanese backgrounds also take part in the Obon Festival. From late June through the month of August, "bon dances" are held at Buddhist shrines around the city to welcome home the spirits of relatives and friends who have died.

Bon dances take place in the churchyard. This style of folk dancing is done to traditional Japanese music. Anyone can take part as long as she or he has a Japanese kimono or "happi coat" (a short version of a kimono). The churches set up booths to sell food and other items.

During June, most Honolulans take special pride in their Hawaiian heritage. On June 11, they celebrate King Kamehameha Day, a special day honoring King Kamehameha the Great. Honolulans place flowers on the statue of King Kamehameha in front of the Judiciary Building in downtown Honolulu. Later, many people take part in or watch a parade with floral floats, marching bands, and all the color of a truly Hawaiian festival. There are also Hawaiian arts and crafts demonstrations, and a street party in Waikiki.

One special part of the King Kamehameha celebrations is the Hula and Chant competition. Some of Hawaii's best hula groups take part in this annual contest to decide who dances the best hula in the islands.

Another favorite Honolulan festival is held in September each year. This is the time of the Aloha Week Festival, a traditional celebration by all of Hawaii's ethnic groups to help preserve the heritage of Hawaii.

This festival honors the history, customs, arts and crafts, music, and dance of early Honolulu. Aloha Week is related to the ancient Hawaiian celebration of *makahiki*, the time when everyone celebrated the harvest season and paid their taxes to the ruling chiefs and kings. At this time the Hawaiians met to play games, hold *luaus* or feasts, and

have a good time after the hard work of harvest time.

Honolulu holds many other ethnic festivals and celebrations each year; few other American cities can claim such a number and variety of cultural celebrations.

While the variety of attractions draw people to Honolulu each year, the beauty of the city and its people keep them here. In recent years, this rapid growth has led to overcrowding.

The city has a housing shortage, and residents are worried that some of the landscape around Honolulu will be destroyed to build more houses, apartments, and hotels. Pollution, too, is another concern. In 1978, Honolulu was voted the cleanest American city of its size. Yet today, residents worry that the increasing number of cars and people in the city may pollute its clean air and water. The number of cars in the city also leads to problems with traffic jams.

As the city government and Honolulans look for a solution to these problems, visitors and islanders alike continue to enjoy Honolulu's beaches, parks, people, restaurants, and everything else the city has to offer. While no longer a royal capital, Honolulu is still filled with the natural beauty and spirit that is a constant reminder of its past. The *aloha aina* of its people will keep Honolulu a "fair haven" for many years to come.

Honolulan young people are taught to respect the city, its people, and its customs.

Places to Visit in Honolulu

Museums

Bernice P. Bishop Museum
1525 Bernice Street
(808) 847-1443

Honolulu Academy of Arts
905 Beretania Street
(808) 538-1006

Iolani Palace
King Street, Downtown
(808) 536-6185

Mission Houses Museum
553 South King Street
(808) 531-0481

U.S.S. *Arizona* Memorial Museum
1 Arizona Memorial Place
(808) 422-2771

Parks

Ala Moana Park
Ala Moana Boulevard

Hanauma Bay Beach Park
Kalanianaole Highway

Kapiolani Park
Kalakaua Avenue

Sea Life Park
Kalanianaole Highway
(808) 259-7933

Waimea Bay Beach Park
Kamehameha Highway, north shore

Special Places

Aloha Tower
Ala Moana Boulevard
Pier 9, Honolulu Harbor
(808) 537-9260

Byodo-In Temple
47-200 Kahekili Highway
(808) 239-8811

Cathedral of Our Lady of Peace
Fort Street Mall, 1184 Bishop Street
(808) 536-7036

Falls of Clyde sailing ship
Pier 7, off Ala Moana Boulevard
(808) 536-6373

Honolulu Zoo
Kapiolani Park
Kapahulu and Kalakaua Avenues
(808) 923-7723

Kawaiaho Church
Punchbowl and King streets
(808) 522-1333

King Kamehameha the Great statue
Aliiolani Hale Judiciary Building
King Street

Pali Lookout over Kailua
Pali Highway
Koolau Mountains

Polynesian Cultural Center
55-370 Kamehameha Highway
(808) 367-7060

The Royal Tomb
Iolani Palace Grounds
King Street

State Capitol
Beretania Street
(808) 548-2211 or (808) 548-6222

Waikiki Aquarium
Kapiolani Park
2777 Kalakaua Avenue
(808) 923-9741

Additional information can be obtained
from these agencies:

Chamber of Commerce of Hawaii
735 Bishop Street
Honolulu, Hawaii 96813
(808) 531-4111

Hawaii Visitors Bureau
2270 Kalakaua Avenue, Suite 801
Honolulu, Hawaii 96815
(808) 923-1811

Honolulu: A Historical Time Line

1778   Captain James Cook discovers Hawaii

1794   William Brown discovers the harbor of Honolulu and names the village "Fair Haven"

1810   King Kamehameha the Great unites the Hawaiian Islands under one kingdom

1819   King Kamehameha the Great dies; his son Liholiho becomes Kamehameha II, ruler of the Kingdom of Hawaii

1820   The first American missionaries arrive in Honolulu

1824   King Kamehameha II dies on a trip to England

1825   The first sugar plantation is started in Manoa Valley, Honolulu

1842   The Kingdom of Hawaii is recognized by the United States

1845   King Kamehameha III moves the capital from Lahaina, Maui, to Honolulu

1850   Honolulu is declared a city and the capital of the kingdom; government allows foreign workers into the kingdom to work on sugar plantations

1887   King Kalakaua gives the United States government rights to use Pearl Harbor as a naval base

1891   King Kalakaua dies; Liliuokalani is proclaimed queen

1893   Queen Liliuokalani is overthrown by American businessmen; the Republic of Hawaii is established under Sanford Dole

1898   Hawaii is annexed by the United States

1900   The Territory of Hawaii is established; fire destroys much of Chinatown

1909	Municipal government of the City and County of Honolulu is formed
1941	Japanese planes bomb Pearl Harbor on December 7; the United States joins World War II
1959	Hawaii is admitted into the Union as the 50th state; jet airplanes begin flying to Hawaii and tourism booms
1970	Jumbo jet service to Honolulu increases tourism. Hawaiian culture and arts experience a new popularity
1976	The Hokule'a, a giant canoe like those used by the ancient Polynesians, sails to Tahiti and returns to Honolulu, proving the early Hawaiian-Polynesian navigation methods
1982	Hurricane Iwa strikes Hawaii, doing much damage to Honolulu and the island of Kauai
1984	Hawaii celebrates the Silver Jubilee (25th anniversary) of its admission to the United States
1985	Honolulu celebrates the 100th anniversary of the arrival of the first Japanese to work on the sugar plantations
1989	Honolulu celebrates the 200-year anniversary of the arrival of the first Chinese immigrants

Index

Aliiolani Hale Judiciary Building, 35, 53
aloha, 11
aloha aina, 12, 55
Aloha Tower, 47

beaches, 18, 44-45
Bishop Museum, 46-47
Brown, William, 24

civil war, 23-24

Diamond Head Crater, 35, 38, 43, 47
Dole, Sanford, 27

East-West Center, 39, 41
education, 41
Eleanora, 23

Hawaiian Islands: formation of, 21; location of, 12; settlers of, 21, 22; statehood and, 31, 33, 43; as a United States territory, 28, 30
"Hawaii Five-O," 31
Hawaiki, 22
Honolulu: as a capital city, 12, 17, 27, 31; celebrations in, 51, 52-53, 55; climate of, 16, 18, 25; conservation in, 22, 25; customs of, 25; ethnic groups in, 13, 15, 23, 24, 25, 26, 30, 33, 38, 48; food in, 48, 49; languages in, 38, 52; location of, 12, 13, 15, 22; missionaries in, 25, 47; names

for, 11, 13, 17, 24, 55; neighborhoods in, 33, 35, 37, 38; official name of, 13, 28; population of, 13, 18, 24, 28, 31, 55; port of, 13, 15, 24; recreation in, 44, 45; settlers of, 13, 21, 22, 23, 24; wildlife in, 18-19, 46
Honolulu Harbor, 23, 24, 28, 47
Honolulu Zoo, 18, 45

industry: agriculture, 15, 25, 27; manufacturing, 15, 25, 27; military, 15, 28, 47; retail, 17, 31; tourism, 13, 18, 31, 43
Iolani Palace, 17, 35, 47

Kaahumanu, 25
Kalakaua, 18, 27
Kalakaua Avenue, 43
Kamehameha I, 23, 24, 25, 27, 35, 53
Kamehameha II, 24
Kamehameha III, 26
Kapiolani Park, 45
kapus, 22
Kawaiahao Church, 25, 35
Kilauea, 21
Koolau Mountains, 16, 37

Liliuokalani, 27

"Magnum, P.I.," 31
Mauna Loa, 21

Mission Houses Museum, 47

National Memorial Cemetery of the Pacific, 37
neighborhoods: Chinatown, 19, 34, 51; Kapahulu, 35; Manoa Valley, 38, 46; Moiliili, 35; Waikiki, 18, 35, 38, 43, 44, 45, 53

Oahu, 12, 13, 19, 22, 23, 24, 27, 38

Pacific Ocean, 12, 13, 19, 21, 31, 44
Paradise Park, 46
Pearl Harbor, 15, 27, 28, 47, 48
pineapple, 15, 16, 25, 27, 38
plantations, 15, 25, 27, 38
Polynesian Cultural Center, 41
Punchbowl Crater, 37

Republic of Hawaii, 27
Royal Kingdom of Hawaii, 17, 24, 27

Sea Life Park, 45
sugarcane, 11, 15, 16, 25, 27, 38

Tantalus Drive, 37, 38

U.S.S. *Arizona*, 47, 48
University of Hawaii at Manoa, 38, 39

Waianae Mountains, 16
Waikiki Aquarium, 45
World War II, 28, 30, 47